A Mourning Heart

Pamela Lawson

Copyright © 2023 by Pamela Lawson

All rights reserved. No part of this book may be reproduced or transmitted in any form or by any means, electronic or mechanical, including: photocopying, recording, or by any information storage and retrieval system, without permission in writing from the copyright owner.

This work is based on the experiences of an individual. Every effort has been made to ensure the accuracy of the content.

A Mourning Heart

Written by Pamela Lawson
Edited by Brenda E. Cortez & Jean Sime
Cover design by Tabassum Hashmi
Interior Layout by Griffin Mill

ISBN: 979-8-9881723-2-1

Published by BC Books, LLC
Franklin, Wisconsin, USA
Brenda E. Cortez, Publisher
Jean Sime, Publishing Coordinator

bcbooksllc.com

Quantity orders can be emailed to: info@bcbooksllc.com

Vector Graphics used courtesy of publicdomainvectors.org

Printed in The United States of America

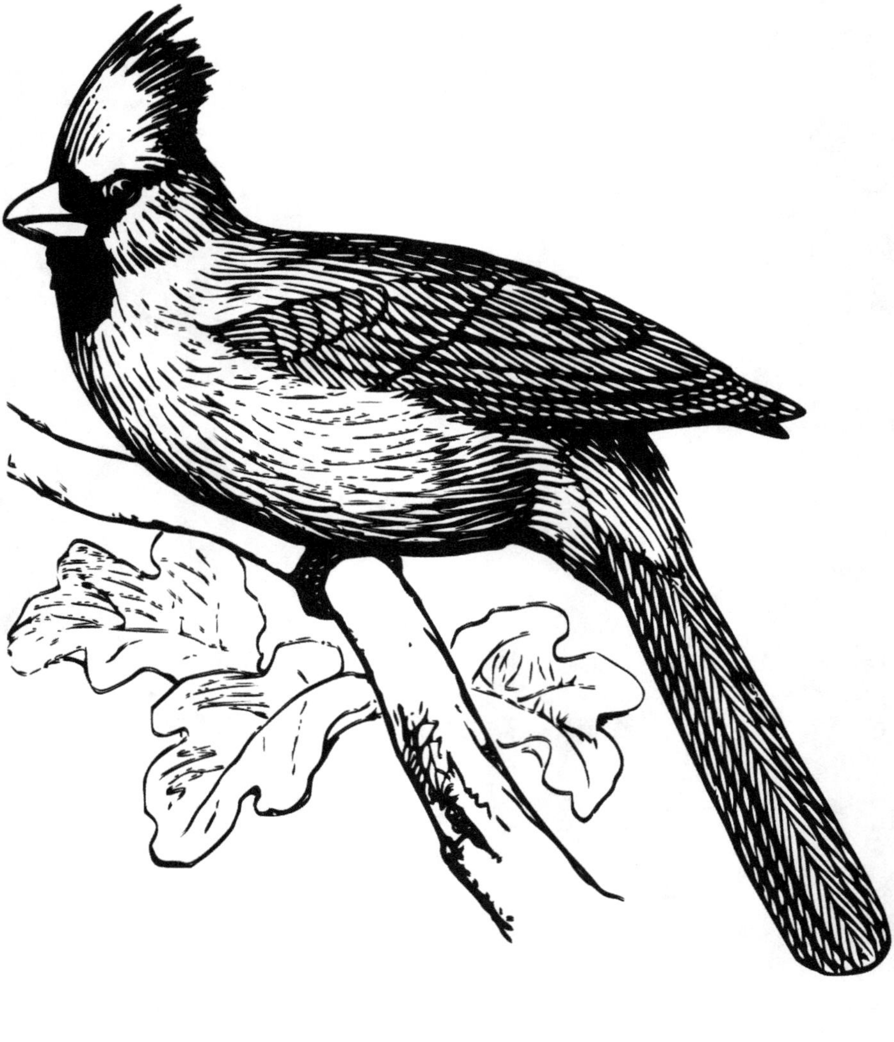

This book of poems is dedicated to our loved ones who are spending eternity in Heaven. It is my sincerest hope that as you read the poems throughout this book, you will find comfort, peace, and love to console the brokenness that exists within your heart.

A love lost is a love that once lived.

INTRODUCTION

When the doctor told my mom there wasn't anything else they could do for her, and she would be placed on hospice care, she knew it meant she was going to die.

It broke my heart because I knew she didn't want to die. She was afraid. She wasn't ready. She was angry. She was tired. She wanted to live. She wanted more time.

As I sat by her bedside, stroking her hair and holding her hand, I did my best to reassure her that we would all be okay, and the last thing she needed to do was worry about those she was leaving behind.

The hospice nurses and aides at Hospice of Chesapeake did everything they could for my sister and me. They listened to us, consoled us, and they let us know our mom wasn't suffering, nor was she in any pain.

Everything happened so quickly. Decisions had to be made in a moment's notice, and information came at us rapidly.

As I sat there with my mom, I thought about the other hospice patients, hoping and praying they had someone by their bed side so they wouldn't pass alone.

I never thought my mom would end up in hospice, but I am glad she was under their care, where they kept a close eye on her and took good care of her.

Even though I wasn't there when my mom took her last breath, I do know with everything I have that she entered God's Heavenly kingdom, and for me, that brings comfort to my heart.

I know my mom did not suffer, and she passed away peacefully under hospice care. For that, I will always be grateful for the care they provided for my mom.

TABLE OF CONTENTS

Your Sorrow	1
From Beginning, to the End	2
In God's Everlasting Light	4
Memory Lane	6
Missing Those We Love	7
Emptiness of Grief	8
You Wonder	9
Memories Shared	10
It is Hard Moving On	11
When You Lose Your Mom	12
Grief Changes Everything	13
Spotlight, Intermission, Encore	14
No Longer am I There	15
A Part of You Always	16
Your Tears	17
Avoiding Grief	18
Keep Living for Those You Lost	19
Everlasting Pain of Grief	20
No Timeline	21
Look Above	22
Celebrate My Life	23
Follow the Brightest Star	24
If Only Heaven Had	25
Your Heart Pays Grief's Cost	26
Memories Keep us Connected	27
Loss is Hard	28
Grief	30
Take All the Time You Need	32

My Heart's Eternal Flame	34
To My Loved One	35
Cancer Does Not Discriminate	36
How Does One Say Goodbye?	39
Don't Let it be too Late	40
Grief is Raw	42
Grieving Regrets	43
Through our Grief	44
A Mama's Hand	45
Angel Wings	47
A Mother's Love	48
Losing a Mother	49
They Say in Time	50
Grief is a Process	52
Love Doesn't End	54
Days, Months, Years are Numbered	55
Fallen Limbs	56
Their Love Lives On	57
A Mom's Love Never Dies	58
I Wonder	59
There Isn't a Rule Book for the Holidays	60
Your Suffering	61
Grieve in Your Own Way	62
Your Dash	64
Feathers	66
My Grandmother's Hands	67
Memory of Your Love	68
When Both Parents are Gone	69
The Struggle of Grief	70
I Saw You	71

Teardrops From Heaven	72
Grieve for Me, But…	73
Alone in My Grief	74
Letter From Your Angel	76
The Healing of Tears	79
God's Chosen One	80
It was My Time	81
Memories	82
Your Love	84
End of Life	85
To Those I Left Behind	86
The Day that Changed Our Lives Forever	87
Don't Think of Me With…	88
Grief Cuts Deep	89
You Lose Them Over and Over Again	90
One of God's Little Angels	91
My Little Angel	92
Missing My Angel	93
More than Just a Memory	94
My Precious Child	95
Forever Connected	96
Love Never Dies	97
Heavenly Angel	98
Welcome Home	100

Your Sorrow

You might think you are alone in your sorrow
and there is no joy in your tomorrows
but in the midst of the pain, you feel
a memory or two will try its hardest
to steal a laugh or a smile from you
to comfort your heart
when it feels lonely and blue.

Grief is difficult to get through
because the life you once knew
has changed in a way you weren't ready for
making your pain hurt even more
tears will fall, catching you off guard
your loss will always hit hard.

They say "time heals" but it never will
because the hole in your heart
will be impossible to fill
you might feel alone in your sorrow
but you will make it through
all of the tomorrows.

From Beginning, to the End

I think about you every day
I think about not being able to share
a thought or a feeling
and how I try different methods
to aid in my healing.

I think about how nights turn into days
and how days turn into nights
I hope and pray that you align signs
directly in my sight, so that I don't miss
a glimmer of your love
that my heart is in need of.

Life changes for those who are left grieving
for what we were accustomed to believing
leaves us questioning so many things
as we try to see the purpose
in what death brings.

Do we lose a life so another can be born?
Does a heart get repaired after it's been torn?

We are told to find comfort
in the memories left behind
but losing someone who meant so much
makes it hard to find
the line that is drawn from beginning to end
when you know without your loved one
you now have to spend.

(con't)

Pamela Lawson

Death is a part of life
and like everything else
memories are like books put on a shelf
only to be read, flipped through,
and shared with others
who will always and forever care
about the legacy
that now has to be carried on
from a love that once lived
who is now, forever gone.

In God's Everlasting Light

The day you left happened so fast
I had hoped the night before
wouldn't be our last
but when that phone call came through
I knew right then I had lost you.

I am now looking up at the sky tonight
in hopes to get a glimpse of you
through Heaven's light
I know you are up there somewhere
I'd give anything to see you standing there.

I want to see your smiling face
I want to feel your love and your grace
I want to be able to feel something good
because if you could have stayed
I know you would.

I want to know what it is like up there
I know you are surrounded by a love
that goes beyond compare
I know you are with those
who went before you
but the pain in my heart
is so hard to break through.

I just want to lay my eyes
upon my angel who took flight
and whose love is now
shining down on me ever so bright
I am lost, I am not going to lie
you are now with the angels
and to you, I had to say goodbye.

(con't)

Pamela Lawson

I know we will be together
when my time comes to an end
and together, forever, we will spend
but until that day comes for me
I want to see your angelic light
and one last time, I want to hold you so tight.

Not having you here hurts my soul
your love is what made my heart whole
I will continue to look up
every day and every night
because I know that is where you are
you are in God's everlasting light.

Memory Lane

When you are missing someone who you love
take a walk down memory lane
a smile will come to you
and for a brief moment
peace is what you'll gain.

As memories bring comfort to your heart
of the time spent
with the one who meant so much
close your eyes
feel their love, their words
and their gentle touch.

Allow your memories to fill
your entire being
allow their memory to fill your soul
allow their memory to make you happy
allow their memory to make you feel whole.

Memories are the window
that proves you cared
they remind you of the love
that was yours and was shared
a love you were so glad you had
will always remember
when you are both happy or sad.

Missing Those We Love

When our loved ones in Heaven
took their place
living life without them
has been very hard to face.

While we know death is a part of life
missing those who meant so much
causes the heart a great amount of strife.
For them we are happy
that no longer are they in pain
but we are also sad because
time with them no longer will we gain.

In life they meant so much
in death they mean even more
and a part of us will always be missing
until we see them again
waiting for us at Heaven's door.

Emptiness of Grief

As you sit and look around
your heart is feeling down
because your loved one you no longer see
that love, that once held your heart's key.

You think about that special someone
all the things they had said and done
you laugh, you smile, your tears begin to flow
as you remember the love that made you grow.

Little things, different scents
remind you of the love you had
and you find yourself feeling sad
you realize, grief just cannot let go
when it comes to certain memories
that is when you know.

Grief is constant, it never goes away
not during the night, nor during the day
hold onto that loved one a little tighter
their love will make your pain a bit lighter.

Grief hurts, and sadly it always will
but when it hits hard, become very still
as love never dies, even when they are gone
their love is what helps carry you on.

You Wonder

When a loved one passes on
and that love is forever gone
you wonder how others can move on so fast
when the grief within you will always last.

You wonder how they can even smile
when your pain just continues to pile
your tears remind you of a love lost
and how those left behind are paying the cost.

You wonder how they can't even say their name
when in your heart their love was your burning flame
saying their name is what you want to hear
that is when you feel your loved one is near.

You wonder how they can ignore their grief
when you can't seem to find any relief
and your entire being so desperately longs
to feel the love that made
your heart beat so strong.

Memories Shared

Memories of a loved one are nice to share
it makes you feel that they are there
memories bring a smile to your face
and those memories make your heart race
memories warm your entire being
and makes their love ever so freeing.

Some memories will make your tears flow
while others will let your laughter glow
there is beauty that's found when you reminisce
about that special someone that you miss
so, share stories every chance you get
as memories are grief's biggest outlet.

It is Hard Moving On

It is so hard moving on
after you lose someone who you love
If you lose a spouse you have to figure out
how to live without them.

Dreams, plans and goals are no longer able
to be reached or set together,
but it doesn't mean they still
can't be kept when you are ready
to reach or set them in their memory.

They would still want you to plan
to celebrate, to dream, to smile,
to laugh, to sing, to dance
and not feel guilty doing so.

Living life without them is excruciating
but their love will give you the strength
the courage, the faith, the hope
to continue living your life
Their life may have come to an end
but yours is still meant to be lived.

When You Lose Your Mom

When you lose your mom
something inside of you shifts
her love, her wisdom, her presence
was always your emotional lift
you knew you could count on her
any time of the day, and for you
she would always go out of her way
the sacrifices she had always made
was a love that was beautifully displayed
for it never mattered if she went without
as long as you were taken care of
that is all she cared about.

A mother's love is without a doubt
one of a kind, and when she is gone
your heart will never find
a love like a mother's love
that's unconditional and true
whose love will always and forever
now be in the heart of you.

Pamela Lawson

Grief Changes Everything

There is no such thing as normal anymore
when your loved one is gone,
the one you were living for
your heart has lost its reason and rhyme
life has lost its momentum,
no longer does it chime.

Everything around you feels strange
as grief makes the familiar change
to you, normal is a thing of the past
your fears now become your daily cast
the pain overrides every other emotion
your tears are your morning and night devotion.

While it's true, things don't feel normal right now
but a new normal, in time
your heart will allow embracing
the new normal will be hard to do
when grief is embedded in the heart of you
just keep an open heart and an open mind
because peace in the new normal
isn't impossible to find.

Spotlight, Intermission, Encore

There will be days when your grief
will take center stage
the spotlight will shine on your every emotion
you will become very anxious
as your emotions will make you feel
as if you're drowning.

You will not be able to catch your breath
your body will shake in fear
your eyes won't see clearly
your heart will beat faster than normal
your body will ache from the pain.

There will be days when your memories will
make you smile and laugh
you will feel an urgency of comfort
and will replay those sweet tender moments
your grief will want an encore
as those memories serve as a purpose of a love
that meant the world to you.

There will be days when you are able to go out
do things around the house
your tears won't flow, your heart won't ache
you will have strength, you will have courage
your grief is needing that intermission.

Wherever you may be at in your grief
in the spotlight, intermission, or an encore
allow yourself to feel, to cry, to do nothing
it is your grief, and it's okay not to be okay.

Pamela Lawson

No Longer am I There

I am no longer there to show you
how much you are loved
but know I am watching you from above
so, you must take care of yourself now
and try to carry on somehow
you must allow yourself to live
and patience with yourself you must give
so, do not give up because I am no longer there
because I will always love you
and for you I will always care.

A Part of You Always

The one you lost is still with you in your heart
in your smile, in your laughter, in your words
in how you carry yourself
and in everything you see…
when you look at the sun, stars, moon
or a rainbow, your loved one is that twinkle
they are the light and the colors
even during the storms.

Your loved one is your calmness
your shelter, no matter what you do
no matter where you go
no matter what you eat
no matter what you drink
no matter what you watch
no matter what you listen to
your loved one is ever so present
the love shared and felt never diminishes
the love shared and felt
will always guide and comfort you.

From your loved one you may be apart
but their love will forever be in your heart
so, on the days you are feeling down
make sure you always look around and
you will most certainly feel their love
because it is you
who they will always be a part of.

Your Tears

When your tears fall
let them
when your tears make your heart ache
let them
when your tears become your voice
let them
when your tears make you feel lost
let them
when your tears make you feel alone
let them
when your tears make you feel weak
let them
when your tears make you feel angry
let them
when your tears make you sad
let them.

Your tears need to be released
to wash away all the yuck
that is within you.

Tears bring healing
tears bring hope
tears bring strength…
release your tears
as often as you need to
just don't allow yourself
to drown in them.

Avoiding Grief

Grief is territorial
people will say the wrong things
they will avoid acknowledging it
and won't understand the depth of your grief.

Say nothing, but be there for those
who are grieving
it means a lot to them
listen to their stories of their loved one
be the shoulder they need to cry on
ask them to tell you about their loved one.

Check on them throughout the day
so, they know they are being thought of
don't dismiss their pain
those who are grieving
want to be seen and heard
you may not know what to say
but your presence means more than you know
to those who are grieving.

Keep Living for Those You Lost

To those who have lost someone
they have loved, whose heart is broken
the familiar is now unfamiliar
the loudness is now quietness
the light is now dark
the plans are now finished
the dreams are now over
just know the unfamiliar is strange
the quietness is stillness
the dark is healing
the plans are to be continued
the dreams are just on hold…

Your journey on earth is not over
live, plan, dream for the love you have lost
your lost loved one wouldn't want you to
stop living, stop planning, stop dreaming…

They are your smile, your laughter, your spark,
your heartbeat, your plans, your dreams…

Keep living for the love you have lost
they wouldn't want it any other way.

Everlasting Pain of Grief

Never feel ashamed
when it comes to your grief
and do not go by anyone's belief
that you should get over how you feel
or in time, your pain will heal
because grief never goes away
you feel it over and over
every waking day, no matter what you do
the grief is still there
grief is something your heart will forever wear
you must relearn everyday
how to live and have patience with yourself
your journey may have changed
but you still must walk your path
even when you feel in your heart grief's wrath
do not let anyone rush your grieving process
because grief over time does not hurt any less.

No Timeline

There is no timeline for grief
nor are there words to bring the griever relief.

Their heart is filled with memories to recall
and their tears will fall with no warning at all.

Never force a griever to move on
let them grieve for a love now gone.

Let them share stories of their greatest love
for they were a blessing to them from God above.

Give them time, give them space
they are the ones who set the pace.

There is no timeline and never will be
as they had to set their loved one free.

Look Above

No matter how broken you will be
when you look at the sky you will think of me
the warmth of the sun will touch your skin
and you will feel my love deep within.

When you see birds, they will be a reminder that
I too, am flying around in the sky above
when you look at the stars in the sky
my love will be the twinkle in your eye
and through the darkness
when the moon shines bright
my love will be your constant light.

The sun will set and it will rise
bringing tears to your eyes
nights will turn into days
and days will turn into nights
my love will always be holding onto you tight.

I will be the breeze
that brushes across your face
I will be each season you will embrace
when I am gone, just look above
the sky will remind you of my love.

Celebrate My Life

Remember me not with your tears
but with a smile for all our years
the life we built was a memorable one
one filled with love, laughter, and fun.

While this is now my time to rest
our life together was one of the best
so, celebrate my life for what it meant
and cherish the years together we had spent.

Celebrate every little thing we had shared
that gave meaning to two hearts who cared
celebrate the milestones that were created
for in our life, they were top rated.

Celebrate the sun, the moon, and the stars
because from your heart I will never be far
celebrate my life, celebrate my love
as I carried your love with me to Heaven above!

Follow the Brightest Star

Each star that shines above
holds nothing but my love
the sparkle is always there
for you and I to share.

From you I did not depart
feel me within your heart
feel the embrace of my wings
and the comfort to you it brings.

Tears flow endlessly from your eyes
knowing each star you see in the sky
has been created just for you
to always and forever see you through.

Make a wish upon a star
I will know exactly where you are
see the special glow now in your sight
I'm flying freely in Heaven's light.

Pamela Lawson

If Only Heaven Had

If Heaven had stairs,
I would visit you every day
and with you for hours I would stay
if Heaven had a phone
I would have you on speed dial
and I would talk to you for the longest while.

If Heaven was closer in my view
my eyes would be able to see you
if Heaven was in my reach
I'd hug you one last time
and for a moment my grief
I wouldn't have to climb.

I know you did your best
to hold on as long as you could
and if you could have stayed longer,
I knew that you would
but I knew you were suffering
I knew you were in pain
and I knew God would make you whole again.

If Heaven is as beautiful as I think it to be
I know you're up there
with the other angels roaming free
and walking in God's beautiful home above
safely secured in His eternal love.

Your Heart Pays Grief's Cost

Grief can look different from day to day
one day you will find that you will cry less
then, the next day you bawl your eyes out
and in your heart, you won't find any happiness.

One day you won't want to do anything
then the next, you will step out on your own
you will want to spend time with those you love
but then, you will want to be left alone.

One day you will feel like you will make it
then the next, you will drop to your knees
you will be consumed with your loss
but their love will put your heart at ease.

One day you will laugh so hard
then the next, your laughter will turn into tears
your emotions will be all over the place
because without any warning, grief switches gears.

Grief is unpredictable and that is okay
you don't owe an apology to anyone
grief can feel like a hurricane
or it can shine as bright as the sun.

Some days will be better than others
So, allow yourself to grieve the love lost
take all the time that you need
because your heart is left with paying grief's cost.

Pamela Lawson

Memories Keep us Connected

I know your tears will constantly flow
because you must let me go
but we will always be a part of one another
and that will never change
just keep doing the things we loved
even though they will feel strange.

I will be beside you every step of the way
my love will be what helps you get stronger
with each passing day
I know how much you will miss me
and in your heart, there is a void
it may seem to you that your life is now destroyed
but our memories will always keep us connected
and my love for you will keep you forever protected.

Loss is Hard

Losing someone we love
is one of the hardest things we must go through
everything changes:
our thoughts, our feelings,
our perspective, our world.

What once was is no longer
plans, dreams, daily routines, are shattered
the pain that exists in our heart
drops us down to our knees
the pain is too much to bear
causing us to question our faith
because we ask:
Why?
How?
Did we do something?
Why them instead of us?

We wish we had more time to say I love you
hold them tighter and longer
do things that were planned
hold conversations
spend time with them.

One never gets over their loss
grieving is a process
everyone grieves differently
and it's okay to cry
grieving does not have a timeline.

(con't)

Pamela Lawson

While life will never be the same
and it forever changes
moving on without them is something
we cannot imagine doing,
but we must allow ourselves at some point to:
smile again, laugh again, find joy again
find happiness again and love again.

We need to draw our strength from God
we need to find comfort in His love
knowing He will help us get through our loss.

We may feel like we won't make it
we may feel like there is no sense for us
to continue to live
we will always have that emptiness inside of us
because of how much we have loved and lost
but our loved ones will always be a part of us
and who we are, and nothing will take that part away.

Grief

There is no time limit when it comes to grief
for some there will never be any signs of relief.

For the love they had lost
there's no amount of time or space
that could bring them any healing
for their loved one could never be replaced.

They will always hold in their hearts
a great amount of sorrow
for what was, will no longer be
for them there are no more tomorrows.

Just give them the time they need
and allow them to feel their pain
because the love they had lost
was their hearts greatest gain.

To those who have loved and lost
I pray for strength, healing, and peace
may you find a reason to laugh and smile again.

Pamela Lawson

Take All the Time You Need

You have lost a loved one
now you are feeling so many emotions
all at once
you want to scream and cry
and even throw things.

You have no idea
how you're going to move forward
and you can't even begin
to think that far in advance
all you know right now is
the pain is heavy
and the pain is hard.

It is okay if you're angry
it is okay if you are lost
it is okay to isolate yourself right now
it is okay for you to mourn what was.

While others get back into their daily routine
it is perfectly fine if you haven't
while others may look like
they have themselves together
it is okay if you do not.

Don't worry if
others expect you to move on
for some, they can't, at least not now
don't worry if
you have more sad days than happy ones
don't worry about other people's opinion
when it comes to YOUR grief.

(con't)

Pamela Lawson

Take all the time you need.

Losing someone you loved
built a life with, or took care of
that love - the love that meant the world to you
that love you had for them never goes away
regardless of how long your loved one has been gone.

My Heart's Eternal Flame

Your memory makes me smile
your absence makes me sad
everything is a reminder
of the years together we had.

All I have are memories
to console me every day
but sometimes that is not enough
as the pain never goes away
you will always be missed
I will always say your name
your love will always be
my heart's eternal flame.

To My Loved One

Not a day goes by
that you aren't thought of
I miss you immensely
the one I will always love.

With me I wish you were here
doing everything we had planned
but for you, God had bigger plans.

His reasoning I still don't understand
but in him I place my trust
for only He knows
when it will be our final call
despite how many tears will fall
together one day I know we will be,
but until then, I will do my best
to live life the only way I know how
until it is my time to be laid to rest.

Cancer Does Not Discriminate

Nobody knows how one will react
when they hear the word cancer
as much as it is hard on the family
to hear their parent has cancer
can you imagine the impact it has
on the person who was diagnosed with it?

First thing that pops in their mind is "death"
but they hold out hope
that their cancer will be curable
and they will be around to live many more years.

But then comes the word treatable
followed by options that could prolong one's life
by weeks, days, even months
then you begin asking if it is worth
putting one's body through radiation
to see if it shrinks
and if it does, should chemo be considered?

But what if they are too frail and too weak
is it worth putting them through the chemo
when we know their body wouldn't be able to handle it?

If the answer is no
then one of the hardest decisions must be made
for the parent who brought you into the world
who you love so very much
despite the complications and the strain
that either crinkled the relationship you have with them
or destroyed the bond once shared
or caused any sort of friction.

(con't)

Regardless of where the line has been drawn
at the end of the day, you only get one Mom or Dad.
Regardless of what was or wasn't said or done
all of that doesn't, or shouldn't, matter
but I know for some, grudges are held
and often they write them off.

Nobody likes to see
those who we love suffering or in pain
we see them deteriorating from cancer
they are no longer able to take care of themselves
or be left alone because they are not stable
when we see them tipping the scale
hospice is the last resort
we have reached the point of
what is in their best interest
being comfortable as can be
and being able to spend what time
they have left with them.

They are nearing the end of their life
and while it is heartbreaking to know
their days are numbered
we need to be mindful
that they too are grieving
and they too are consumed
with fear, sadness, heartache
as they are facing and fearing the unknown.

They worry about the wellbeing
of those who will be left behind
they may have their own list of regrets
they may feel like they didn't do enough on earth
they may feel they have let people down
they grieve what was
and what they know is coming
they do not know what will happen
to them when they pass;   (con't)

will they be Heaven bound or be sent to Hell
they have their own set of questions and doubts
they are entitled to grieve
as they are overwhelmed with the process.

All we can do in their final days
is to continue to lift their spirits
say whatever needs to be said
and make whatever amends that are needed
and let them know it is okay for them to pass
never in my wildest dreams
did I ever think my sister and I
would be in the position
to make a decision like this for our mom.

Her days were numbered
the census was she would pass
at the end of the week
while I knew there wasn't a crystal ball
that predicted one's date or time of death
but the thought of being told she would pass
at the end of this week hit hard
I didn't feel comfortable going to work
and my mom wanted me to stay the night
because she was so scared.

I have always been one to put work first
but when it comes to family
my family is my number one priority.

Everyone has an expiration date
no life is safe, so love always, forgive more
and let go of grudges, because life is way too short
and life with those you love
is something that is precious and priceless.

How Does One Say Goodbye?

How does a child, no matter their age
say goodbye to their parents
who will be taking their place
in God's Heavenly Kingdom?

A lot needs to be said
but where does one start?

You say how much you love them
you let them know they will be missed
you share the stories they shared
with you a million times
you say everything to them
that was never said
you apologize to them
for not being as present
as you know you should have been
you tell them they don't have to worry anymore.

You tell them it is okay for them to go
when you say everything to them
that you needed to say
and you have nothing else that needs to be said.

You hold their hand
you kiss their forehead
you rub their head.

You sit in silence
and just be there with them
you find moments of laughter and smiles
until the flood gates open and all you can do is cry.

As painful as it is
the greatest gift you can give them is comfort
and all you can do now is wait
wait for them to pass.

Don't Let it be too Late

No matter what, in life
there will be regrets
especially when someone you love passes on.

If only we said I love you more
if only we spent more time
if only we didn't argue
if only we called more often
if only we were more compassionate
if only we were more kind
if only we were more forgiving
if only we did more
if only we would have noticed
if only we saw the signs
if only we were more present
if only we put ourselves in their shoes
if only we took the time to listen
if only we were more caring
if only we were more understanding

All the what ifs cause us more pain
because in the end
what we did or didn't say
are things we can't take back
and are things we left unsaid.

We thought we had more time
to make amends, to do better, to be better
but what I have come to realize is…
"A life of no regrets is a life without lessons learned."

But we fall back into our routines
we go about our days
planning and rushing
not having enough time
pushing those we love to the side.   (con't)

Pamela Lawson

And when the time rolls around again
we are left with regrets, tears
heartaches, guilt, and our grief
and the what ifs play continuously
on repeat once again.

Maybe one day we will get it
maybe one day we will realize
the importance of living
not for material things, but for quality time
to make and create memories with those we love.

Grief is Raw

Grief makes us reflect on our actions
our words and our feelings
grief breaks every ounce of our being
grief makes us feel alone and lost.

We are forced into a path
that isn't familiar to us
As we embark on a journey of grief
we cannot lose sight of the love
and memories one shared
we need to be thankful and blessed
that the love that is now at rest
was and will always remain a part of
who we are.

Every step we take moving forward
every beat that our heart makes.
every smile that shows up on our face.
Every laugh that comes from deep within
is a constant reminder of the love once felt
and is still shared by those left behind.

When we stop remembering
and saying their name
is when we lose them forever.

Grieving Regrets

Hold no regrets in your heart
when someone you love dies
because no matter how much time wasn't spent
you will always think otherwise.

If only you did this, that, or the other
then your regrets would be
less of a bother
no matter how many negative thoughts
are in your head.

Remember how lucky you were
to have them in your life
always remember the good times
and the funny ones too.

The many things you learned from them
and how much they meant to you
you will never get over the loss
because of the impact of their love
in your life they had played.

So, let go of the should haves
could haves and the would haves
because a difference in your life
they have made.

Through our Grief

Grief is something that never goes away
we just learn to live with it every day.

It doesn't get easier as time passes by
no matter how hard we try.

Grief remains very much a part of
the hole that is left in our heart
and all we can do through our grief
is rely on memories to bring us
a small amount of relief.

A Mama's Hand

A Mama's hand
is the first hand you will hold
and what will guide you no matter how old.

A Mama's hand
is a hand full of love
and so much more than you ever thought of.

A Mama's hand
is a hand of great strength
will go to great lengths.

A Mama's hand
you will hold in the end
before God calls her home
where in eternity she will spend.

A Mourning Heart

Angel Wings

I think about you every day
the sadness won't go away
I think about your living years
and it brings so many tears.

I think about so many things
especially the day you got your angel wings
oh, how happy you must have been
when Heaven's gates you entered in.

Awaited you were no more sorrows
no more days and no more tomorrows
to be reunited with those who had gone before
was what your heart had longed for
a beautiful soul to Heaven had flown
and now you have angel wings of your own.

A Mother's Love

A mother's love never dies
even when she is gone
her love is embedded in our heart
which helps us carry on.

A mother's love shines ever so bright
even when she is gone
her love is still our guiding light.

A mother's love
is a blessing from above
a love we will always think of.

Even when she is gone
as nothing compares
to a mother's endless love.

Losing a Mother

The pain of losing a mother
will never go away
we will miss her every single day.

The little things will remind us of
everything she had done
carried out by her love.

She will never be gone
in our heart she will forever be
hold onto the memories
and it will be her
we will always see.

They Say in Time

They say in time I will be okay
and the grief I feel will go away
but I do not think that is true
because I will always miss you.

They say you are in a better place
and with them I agree,
but knowing you are gone
is hard to embrace.

No matter what others say
to comfort the pain
I feel the hole in my heart
will never heal.

Pamela Lawson

Grief is a Process

Grief is one of the hardest things
in life we must bear
it is challenging, it is intense
and it is overwhelming.

Grief is a process
it's your grief and nobody else's
when you lose someone who you love
people don't often know what to say or do
they can only send their condolences
they say time will heal
and just focus on the happy times
don't be sad, for they are in a better place
while these can bring some comfort
often, they do not.

You will learn how to
deal with the loss of your loved one
you will learn how
to navigate through the grief
you will learn how to
live without the one you had lost
you will learn in time.

When grief is fresh
so many emotions come to the surface
allow yourself to feel
every emotion that consumes you
don't think for one minute
you have to suppress your feelings
for the sake of others.

Don't think for one minute
you have to put on a happy face to benefit others
don't think for one minute
there is a particular way to grieve, there isn't.   (con't)

It is okay to cry, to be sad, to be mad,
to be angry, to be frustrated
and to feel numb for however long
don't allow others to dictate your grieving journey.

Anger is a part of grieving
you may find yourself angry at yourself
you may feel regrets for not being there
when your loved one transitioned
maybe you got into an argument
maybe you are angry at God
for not healing the one you've lost
maybe you are angry at the doctors
maybe you feel they didn't do enough
maybe you are angry at the one you lost
for not going to the doctor or hospital.

Share with God how you're feeling
and where in your grieving you are at
He already knows how you feel
but He wants you to come to Him.

Just remember, God never intended
for our hearts to suffer grief
He gave us His word to help us through it.

Psalm 34:18 says, "The Lord is close
to the brokenhearted and saves those
who are crushed in spirit."

God understands our grief and
He promises to be with us
to comfort us with His word,
and to give us
"Peace that transcends all understanding."
(Philippians 4:7)

Just know, in your grief you are not alone.

Love Doesn't End

It does not matter how long
someone has been gone
their presence still exists
within our heart
they were someone we loved
who gave meaning to our life
and to the world
just because they are no longer here
doesn't mean we stop thinking about them
nor does it mean we stop loving them
Grief is a love that once was and will always be.

Days, Months, Years are Numbered

If you were told you only had a few months to live
would there be anything you would want to give
in the time you had left to those you love
before you took your place in Heaven above?

Would you wish for anything
or would you be satisfied
with the life you had lived
one lived with so much pride
would you say anything or nothing at all
or would you let all your tears fall?

Would you be angry, would you be sad
or would you be thankful
for the years you have had
is knowing better than not knowing
or would you give up or keep on going?

How does one wrap their mind
around the fact that they are dying
receiving this kind of news is terrifying
we all have an expiration date
but when someone you love
has been told they only have
a certain amount of time left
all we can do is pray to the dear Lord above
that during what time they have left
no pain or suffering will take place
and their love during this time
is ours to continue to embrace.

Fallen Limbs

Another limb has fallen off our family tree
someone who meant the world to me
their limb may be broken
but their love forever remains
my loss is now one of Heaven's
most beautiful gains.

As new branches grow
and begin to take their place
we remember the fallen limbs
with a smile upon our face.

They filled out our family tree
with their beauty and their grace
so let me no longer grieve
for the fallen limbs
as their memory in my heart
will always be life's most beautiful hymn.

Pamela Lawson

Their Love Lives On

For those who have lost a loved one
and the grief is unbearable
keep saying their name
keep thinking about them
share their memory
cherish the time you had with them
be grateful for the times they were in your life.

They may be gone
but their love lives on in you
and through you
I talk to you every day
but that is nothing new
you're always on my mind
and in my prayers too.

What makes it so hard losing you
is knowing you are never coming back
and that hurts even more
which makes my grief higher stacked.

Your life in my heart has left its mark
a life I will never forget for the rest of my days
a life that meant to me so much
through my grief, your love, I will always praise.

A Mom's Love Never Dies

Mom, I know you are watching over me
from your new home
I can feel you near
as I am surrounded by your love.

I see your smile in the morning sun
I feel your hug in the gentle breeze
I hear your laughter
when I see the cardinals in the trees
and when day turns into night
and the stars fill the sky
I feel the warmth of your love
a love in my heart that won't ever die.

Pamela Lawson

I Wonder

I look at the birds flying in the sky
as the clouds slowly drift by
I wonder if you can feel my love
in your Heavenly home above.

I wonder if you see my tears fall
as our memories I often recall
I wonder if you can sense my loneliness
and how my pain doesn't hurt any less.

I wonder if you know how much you are missed
and how in my heart a void now exists
I wonder if you hear me say your name
and how my life no longer feels the same.

I wonder if you see me through the sun
the stars, and the moon
I wonder if you will send me signs anytime soon
I wonder a lot of things every day and night
since you crossed over into Heaven's light.

There Isn't a Rule Book for the Holidays

During the holidays there isn't a rule book
with how grief around this time should look
some will celebrate, while others may not
the holidays trigger one's grief a lot.

Decorations aren't as welcoming as before
Christmas carols don't hold
the same meaning anymore
traditions don't feel the way they used to
making the holidays harder to get through.

The holidays at one point were full of cheer
but for those left grieving
it is a sad time of the year
so, please be patient, let their tears fall
as holidays of the past, they will recall
memories that filled their heart with love
are now holiday memories
they will always think of.

Your Suffering

To those whose hearts are broken
and your tears continue to fall
where no break has happened in between
and peace is something you cannot recall.

Just know you are going through a season
a season where you cannot catch your breath
where your heartache has no rhyme or reason
just know God feels everything you feel
and He knows you are suffering a lot
but the one thing you need to remember is
alone during your heartache
is something you are not.

Grieve in Your Own Way

Never tell someone how they should grieve
or tell them what they should believe
everyone has the right to grieve in their own way
and in their grief no matter how long
they have the right to stay.

Let them feel their grief and all its stages
there is no timeline nor guidelines per any pages
their grief is theirs and theirs alone
as they are left with a heartache
they wish they've never known.

Choose your words wisely to a grieving soul
because no longer do they feel whole
sit with them in their time of sorrow
and pray over them for a brighter tomorrow.

Pamela Lawson

Your Dash

It is never easy saying, "See you later"
to someone you love or who had a huge impact
not only in your life
but in your heart as well.

Instead of worrying, pray
instead of crying, laugh
instead of hating, love
instead of gossiping, walk away
instead of being sad, smile.

Remember:
God gave us arms to hug
God gave us a voice to stand up for others
God gave us hands to help others
God gave us a smile to brighten lives
God gave us families and friends to love.

Their footsteps have stopped
their heartbeats no longer beat
their laughter is now silent
their smiles are now at rest
but their love is ever so present
in the heart of you.

We all have a beginning and an end
and do not know when ours will end
so, the dash in between
make sure you follow your dreams
show empathy toward others,
be kind to everyone,
and love unconditionally

(con't)

Make your dash rewarding
not to yourself but for others
make your dash meaningful
not for yourself but to others.

Make your dash memorable
not for yourself but those in your inner circle
because when it is your time
and you are being remembered
it is that in between that matters the most.

Feathers

Feathers are something we don't often see
but when one is found, they are precious as can be
feathers symbolize so many wonderful things
and a special meaning is what they bring.

It could be a sign from Heaven above
sent to us from someone we love
it could be a sign for us to take flight
seeing all the possibilities that are in our sight.

If a feather crosses your path
it was Heaven sent
and for just you it was meant
maybe you had prayed for some kind of sign
or perhaps, you needed some encouragement
from a higher divine
a feather holds a spiritual connection
a blessing of protection, direction, and reflection.

Pamela Lawson

My Grandmother's Hands

When I looked at my grandmom's hands
they were hands of a life's master plan
her hands were instrumental
and played an integral part
as they created a beautiful work of art.

Her hands took care of those she loved
her hands always prayed to God above
her hands carried things heavy and light
they provided comfort for others day and night.

Her hands baked, cooked, and created
in her lifetime they were perfectly illustrated
her hands told a story, such beauty to behold
though they were wrinkled, weak and old.

Her hands served herself and others very well
they embraced life as everyone could tell
I will always remember
the hands of my grandmother
because they resembled dedication,
warmth and love like no other.

Memory of Your Love

My heart reminisces of the years you were here
and wonderful memories of your love appears
they console my tears as they lift my spirits high
your memory brings me peace like the clouds in the sky.

I feel nothing but warmth in the memories that I recall
they comfort me when my tears begin to fall
time will never erase the pain I feel
nor will time ever be able to heal.

The void that now exists in this heart of mine
your memory like the sun will always shine
you will never be forgotten as long as I live
because love is what your memory gives.

When Both Parents are Gone

I am an adult who has lost both of her parents
I can no longer call them
I can no longer talk to them
I can no longer hear their voices
I can no longer hear their laughter
I can no longer see them on holidays
I can no longer celebrate special occasions with them
I can no longer tell them I love you
I can no longer hug them
I can no longer share things with them.

The "I can no longer" thoughts
weigh heavy on my heart
I thought I would have had them around longer
I would always say, "I will see them,
I will spend time with them, I will talk to them"
on all the tomorrows, but time ran out.

We always think we will have tomorrow
but tomorrow isn't promised to anyone
no matter how busy you are
no matter how tired you may be
no matter what is going on in your life
always make time for your parents
before the "I can no longer"
weighs heavy on your heart
and all the tomorrows become too late.

The Struggle of Grief

The other day I went to my parent's resting place
and I am still struggling to embrace
the loss my heart has been left to bear
and I do not think I will ever get there.

When it comes to healing
because it hurts so much
as the loss is still fresh
and unbearable to touch
maybe one day I will be able to
let go of the pain, but for now
my heart has been left with a heavy stain.

There is no room for anything else
but the grief I feel
and I am trying to find the strength to deal
with the fact they are gone forever
never coming back
now I must figure out how to move on
with this huge impact
that has changed my life forever
and changed the game,
since my life without my parents
will never be the same.

I Saw You

I saw you standing by my grave
I saw your tears as they came in waves
I heard the sadness in your voice
you know I would have stayed if I had a choice.

I heard everything you said
I felt your every pain
I know you would give anything to see me again
I saw you standing by my grave
I heard the heartfelt message to me you gave.

If only you could hear me
you would hear me say:
"My love is always with you,
I am with you every day
for me do not grieve
it is time to put your grief to rest
I know it is hard, but you must try your best
you still have a life to live, so live it for me
and with you every step of the way
is where I'll be."

I saw you standing by my grave
I hope you felt the kiss on your cheek I gave
I watched as you walked away from my grave
I hope you heard me whisper,
"This is now your time to be brave."

No matter how long we will be apart
I will always be close to you
just feel me in your heart.

Teardrops From Heaven

When teardrops fall from Heaven above
the angels are missing the ones they love
even though they are always nearby
they too have times when they cry.

They know they cannot be there
to hold and kiss the ones they care
nor can they see their loving face
their footsteps they now do trace.

No matter how hard they try
they will never be able to say goodbye
to the family and friends they have left behind
their love is etched within their mind.

So, when you feel their teardrops fall
memories are what the angels recall
of the times they had while on earth
that gave to their heart's great worth
so, when you look toward the sky
hear the angel's heartfelt reply
through each teardrop that you feel
their love for you is very much real.

Grieve for Me, But…

Grieve for me just for a little while
but think of me with a smile
focus on the good times we had
and let not your heart be sad.

Grieve for me if you must
but let your tears turn into dust
from you I will never be gone
through you my memory lives on.

Grieve for me but be at peace
let your sadness be what you release
you don't want to hold in your grief
I know, you too, need that relief.

Grieve for me, but continue to live
you still have so much to give
pick up where I left off
and continue my journey
and live your life, if not for you, for me.

Grieve for me, but grieve in love
and look for me in the skies above
I am now an angel, and I am yours
where my love will be your everyday cure.

Alone in My Grief

Alone in my grief is where I sit
my emotions all over the place
my heart is broken in two
inside of me is an empty space.

No one will be able to fill the void
no words can heal the pain I feel
I am lost without you
I cannot believe this is real.

I look at pictures and my memory recalls
every smile you made
I can hear your laughter
as if with me you are still here
in the mornings, the nights, and the days after.

I find myself not being able to let you go
I am afraid if I do, the distance between us
will only continue to grow
and while I know you are in my heart
it doesn't take away the fact
my life has been torn apart.

My tears will flow, they always will
no matter how many years come and go
I will miss you
still my grief is a hard road to cross
I must figure out how to deal with my loss.

Pamela Lawson

Letter From Your Angel

To my family and to my friends
God told me I should write you a letter
so, I thought I'd write even though I know
it will not make any of this better
but perhaps it would if only for a second
ease some of the pain
that has caused the strength within your heart
impossible to regain.

There is no more suffering or sadness here
in His Heavenly home above
My journey is now over
and I wanted to let you know
I am secure in God's love
with arms opened wide
He welcomed me and said,
"Welcome home my child"
I could not help but stand in total awe
when He looked at me and smiled.

He told me to follow Him
but in the midst of my footsteps
I froze because I knew once I crossed over
the Heavenly gates would close
and those who I love and care about
would be on the other side
with mixed emotions of sadness, of anger
of resentment and of pride.

After a minute or two I told God
I was finally ready to go
He led me through the gate
and that is when my tears began to flow
for I knew I would be leaving
my family and my friends behind
with only memories of me in their heart
and in their mind.

(con't)

This letter isn't easy for me to write
but it was something I had to do
so, as you are reading this
know I am reading this along with you
let my words in this letter be
in some small way a comfort zone,
especially during the times
when you feel sad, lonely, and alone.

Please know from your life I am not gone
I am very much still there
my love can be felt in everything you do
it can be felt everywhere
and while it is true
my memory will cause you to cry some days
never forget that my love will
comfort you in so many different ways.

Whatever you do, don't think your life
isn't worth living anymore
you still have a lot to do
and a lot of things to be thankful for
let your heart not be filled with pain
or filled with sorrow, but find it in your heart
to live and look forward to tomorrow.

And that may be something right now
you can't imagine to do
but know I will be there
every step of the way with you
so do not think this letter was written
to you as a final good-bye
it was written to soothe and to comfort
the tears in your eyes.

(con't)

A Mourning Heart

Together again someday we will be
but until that day arrives, enjoy, embrace
and cherish the rest of your life
do not think for a minute
I wouldn't want it any other way
because life is meant to be lived
to its fullest every day.

Pamela Lawson

The Healing of Tears

When you think about me
I know you still grieve
don't be sad in your heart
you need to believe
that even though I am not there
my presence can still be felt
so don't think in life a bad hand
is what you have been dealt.

Things happen in life
we cannot comprehend or explain
but sometimes things do happen
that cause us a great amount of pain
for some, time never heals the loneliness
or the sadness that exists
but there isn't anything wrong
with taking the time to reminisce.

For that time is very much needed
to bring to the heart healing
don't be afraid of the emotions
during this time, you will be feeling
memories are what brings loved ones closer
to the heart's core and memories
are what keeps their love present even more.

So, the next time tears fall because of a memory
embrace every single one
for they represent times of happiness
that were filled with laughter and with fun
and even though there will be days
when the memories will be too painful to recall
for the healing process to begin
the tears are what need to fall.

God's Chosen One

God called me home today
as it was my time to go
do not allow your tears to continue to flow
as I am now at rest, free from all the pain
no longer am I suffering
so, there is no need for you to be sad.

I did all I could do on earth while I was there
I had handled everything God placed in my care
while I was on earth, I had done for God my part
so according to His plan, it was my time to depart.

Sometimes lives end way before their time
why this happens nobody knows
but it doesn't mean life for those
who have been left behind has to come to a close
as death is not the end, it's a new beginning
so, for me please do not grieve
because the day I was called home
a new beginning is what I received.

This is now my time to rest
as my work on earth has been done
do not worry, do not fear, do not doubt
and do not cry
as I was God's chosen one.

Pamela Lawson

It was My Time

Do not allow your sorrow
to rob you of your tomorrows
just look above at the clouds
and, for me, feel nothing but proud.

As God made the final call
even though He knew your tears would fall
I know you think He took me too soon
and you didn't hear the angel's sweet angelic tune.

It was time for me to depart
and I too, feel the sadness in your heart
just look for me in each sunset and in each sunrise
and let my love be the sparkle in your eyes
from you, I will never be gone
even though it was my time to move on.

Memories

When you lose someone who you love
you seek answers from God above
in hopes He will shed some light
as to why He didn't make things right.

And when the answers remain unknown
that is when the heart feels that much more alone
the tears flow like there is no tomorrow
for the heart is filled with so much sorrow.

You think you won't make it, but in time you will
you just cannot allow yourself
to come to a complete standstill
it doesn't mean you have to forget
you must find the strength to move on
the memories that were created over the years
will never be gone.

There's nothing wrong with shedding tears
when something comes to mind
but in your heart, you too must find
the happiness, the joy, the laughter
that your loved one has left behind
for their time here on earth
was a very precious one
So do not think about what you
should've or could've done.

Instead, bask in the time that was spent
between the both of you
because that is what your loved one
would want you to do
remember the good times you both had
and a smile will shine through
no longer will you feel sad
let your memories be what comforts you   (con't)

Pamela Lawson

every second, minute, hour of the day
because the one you love is still with you
every step of your way.

Your Love

Your love continues to guide us
on the darkest, cloudiest days
your love continues to comfort us
when our pain in our heart stays.

Your love continues to make us smile
on the days when we are sad
your love continues to make us laugh
when our days and nights are bad.

Your love continues to sparkle
like the stars that fill up the sky
your love continues to be our light
your love was special and that is no lie.

Your love for us was one of a kind
a love we miss every single day
your love held all of us together
and kept so many things at bay.

Your love meant the world to us all
and even though you're no longer here
your love will always be our centerpiece
a love we will celebrate every day
throughout every year.

Pamela Lawson

End of Life

End of life is a hard thing to process
knowing they'll be at peace
doesn't make it hurt any less
reminiscing about the good times had
doesn't take away how much we are sad.

Seeing those we love waiting for them
to take their last breath
makes us feel so many emotions
at their time of death
end of life makes us question so many things
and all the feelings this stage brings.

But one thing our hearts come to realize
that no matter what
time never dries the tears from our eyes
the pain is something indescribable
that we, ourselves become unrecognizable
the end of life for our loved ones
means so much more
for when they take that last final breath
God is waiting to welcome them
through Heaven's door.

To Those I Left Behind

To the loved ones I left behind
I hope you keep some things in mind
my love will always be around
my love will keep you safe and sound.

My love will console the tears you cry
and I hope you know this isn't goodbye
for now, we just had to part ways
and while there may be for you hard days.

May you always feel my presence around
and our memories lift you up
when you're feeling down
as much as you miss me, I miss you too
my love will always be in the heart of you.

This is now my time to rest
and you have a life to live
you still have so much yet to give
miss me, grieve for me just for a little while
but always remember me with a smile.

The Day that Changed Our Lives Forever

The day we had to say goodbye to you
was very hard for us to get through
you were our last parent standing
and now our tears, they are still landing
on the pain we feel every day and night
we are still grieving your loss
which has no end in sight
what once was familiar no longer remains
nothing but sadness running through our veins.

Time will never dry our tears
time will never heal our loss
being able to go on without you
will be a hard road to cross
as much as we know
you wouldn't want us to grieve
the fact you are gone is still hard to believe
we are doing our best, that is all we can do
but we are still trying to figure out
how to live without you.

Don't Think of Me With…

Don't think of me with sadness
don't think of me as being gone
think of me with love in your heart
and keep my memory living on.

Don't think of me with tears
don't think of me with continued grief
think of me with loving thoughts
that bring to your heart some relief.

Don't think of my passing with anger
don't think of my passing with dread
think of me with smiles and laughter
where memories were created
that brings comfort instead.

Don't think of my passing as a life lost
don't think of my passing as an ending
think of my passing as a new beginning
because in eternity is where I am spending.

Grief Cuts Deep

Grief cuts, it cuts deep
it is ours alone to keep
the emotions are raw
so raw that we withdraw.

Grief is just that
there are no signs of relief
we try to stand but we fall
leaving us with nobody to call.

We try to rise, rise above the loss
of the one we love
no escape from the pain we feel
and time, time does not heal.

No matter what anyone says
grief affects us in different ways
there is no getting through it
the longer they are gone, the harder it gets.

There are no antidotes
for anyone left grieving
so, when it is our time
we will be reunited
and that my friend, is worth believing.

You Lose Them Over and Over Again

Every time you think about them
you lose them again
every time you share a memory
you lose them again.

Every celebration or holiday
you lose them again
traditions once done together
you lose them again.

A life that once loved, cared,
smiled, laughed, cried, sang,
danced, and breathed
is a life that will always be missed
is a life that will always be grieved
is a life that will always mean something.

Just because they are no longer here
doesn't mean those left behind
cannot and should not mourn.

Regardless how long they lived
a day, a week, a month or years
they were a part of our love
our journey, our growth
so no, time will never heal
a love that meant so much
to someone and to everyone.

One of God's Little Angels

God gave one of his little angels
an important job to do
he sent her down to earth
to love and look after you
she catches every tear that falls
she listens to your memories
no matter how big or how small.

She sits beside you softly
quietly holding your hand
when your grief is raw
and too hard to withstand
she provides you with comfort
she has a heart full of love
she is your little angel
she is a blessing from above.

Talk to her, let her know how you feel
little by little she will help you adjust
and she will help you to heal
she is one of God's little angels
so, handle her with care
because when you need her the most
she will always be there.

My Little Angel

Oh, my little angel, how I miss you so
it broke my heart the day you had to go
I know you look beautiful
in your little angel wings
I know love and joy to the other angels
Is what you bring.

I can hear your laughter as clear as day
it warms my heart in every possible way
in my heart I know you are with me still
despite I had to let you go against my will.

My little angel, oh how I feel your love
as you look down on me from high above
my tears for you have a constant flow
the pain hurts so much from here down below.

The day I lost you was the hardest day of all
you didn't get a chance to grow up
you were still so very small
God needed you
and you were called up to his throne
even though it meant I would be alone.

There is a hole no one can ever fill
as time for me comes to a stand still
you will always be my little angel,
who meant so much to my heart
my love for you will always be
even though we are apart.

Pamela Lawson

Missing My Angel

I wish I could pay my angel a visit
the one who I greatly miss
I would hug her in a tight embrace
and on her cheek, I would plant a kiss.

I would tell her all the things
I didn't get a chance to say
I would tell her how much I love her
and how much she meant to me
I would make amends and share all my regrets
if only it was my angel that I could see.

One day we'll be together
although I do not know when
I will send messages to my angel above
and pray she hears my every word
for she will always be my angel
the one I will forever love.

More than Just a Memory

You will never be just a memory
you will always be here with me
all the things we would say and do
will always make me think of you.

You are someone who will never be replaced
your love always brought a smile to my face
you are more than a memory
you were my special one
and everything about you
was brighter than the sun.

You warmed this heart and soul of mine
your love gave my life a beautiful design
you may be gone, but for me,
you will always remain
an important part of me.

You are more than just a memory
you were my greatest love
you were and will always be
a blessing to me from above.

My Precious Child

I see your smiling face in my dreams
oh, how you left way too soon
I hear your laughter as I gaze up
at the sun, the stars and the moon.

The pain of losing you cuts deep
but in my heart is where you'll always be
my precious child, everything inside of me
is missing everything about you,
it hurt me to set you free.

But there is no doubt in this heart of mine
you are up in Heaven shining your light
and I know you are doing just fine
from me you will never be out of sight.

I will always grieve for you
my precious child
the child I held in my arms
the one I will always love
it is true, for now we are apart
but you are my angel
who is watching from above.

My precious child, in my heart you live on
and that brings comfort to this heart of mine
because from me you will never be gone
as long as I live, my precious child,
you will always shine.

Forever Connected

When our loved ones go before us
it is so hard to imagine
living life without them, but
knowing we are forever connected
brings our heart some solace.

No matter what milestones
we celebrate or achieve
our loved ones celebrate with us
in spirit they celebrate
holidays, birthdays, anniversaries,
graduations, and births.

Our loved ones share our excitement,
our tears, and our joy
death may separate us from them
but the love shared
keeps us connected forever.

I know your tears will constantly flow
because you had to let me go
but we will always be a part of one another
and that will never change
just keep doing the things we loved
even though they now feel strange.

I will be beside you every step of the way
my love will be what helps you get stronger
with each passing day.

I know how much you miss me,
and in your heart, there is a void
it may seem your life is now destroyed
but our memories will keep us connected
and my love for you will always
keep you forever protected.

Love Never Dies

Our loved ones know
we miss them every day
but they do not want us
grieving our life away
for us, the sun rises and still sets
every day, another chance is what we get.

For us, the sun, the moon, and the stars
are a reminder that from us, they are not far
their love is a beacon of light
that in our life shines bright.

Seasons come and go,
but their love gives our heart
a warm and special glow
for us, their journey we need to carry on
because from us they are not gone
the love never dies
it still exists in the heavenly skies.

Heavenly Angel

I wish I could see what Heaven looks like
so, I knew you were all right
but I have a good feeling
you're probably dancing and singing
in God's everlasting light.

I wonder what it was like
when the angels escorted you in
you were probably the happiest
you have ever been
how joyous it must have felt
going home to be with the Lord
one of life's greatest rewards.

I am sure you're flying around
since you have been Heaven bound
oh, how I wish I could see
the smile on your face
since you are now an angel
in God's heavenly home
a magnificent and splendid place.

Pamela Lawson

Welcome Home

Well done and welcome home
my faithful one
I am proud of all you have done
you shined your light at all times
and you shined it bright.

You built a bridge of love, not a bridge of hate
a pathway for others you did create
it is now up to them to follow where it leads
and plant along their way even more seeds.

It is up to them to choose
if they will plant them or not
as love brings comfort to those
who are suffering a lot
you loved with all your heart
and you did your earthly part
welcome home my child,
here you have gained your wings
you left behind your footprints
where in life that is a beautiful thing.

Just because our loved ones pass on
and take their place in Heaven
does not mean their love passes with them.

Our loved ones lived,
they breathed, they mattered
our loved ones still live,
breathe and matter in us and to us
our loved ones will always and forever
give our life purpose.

(con't)

Pamela Lawson

They will always bring to us
and to our heart a smile,
a laugh, a song and a dance
their love will always be a beautiful love,
a love we were blessed with
and a love that forever lives on in us
and through us.

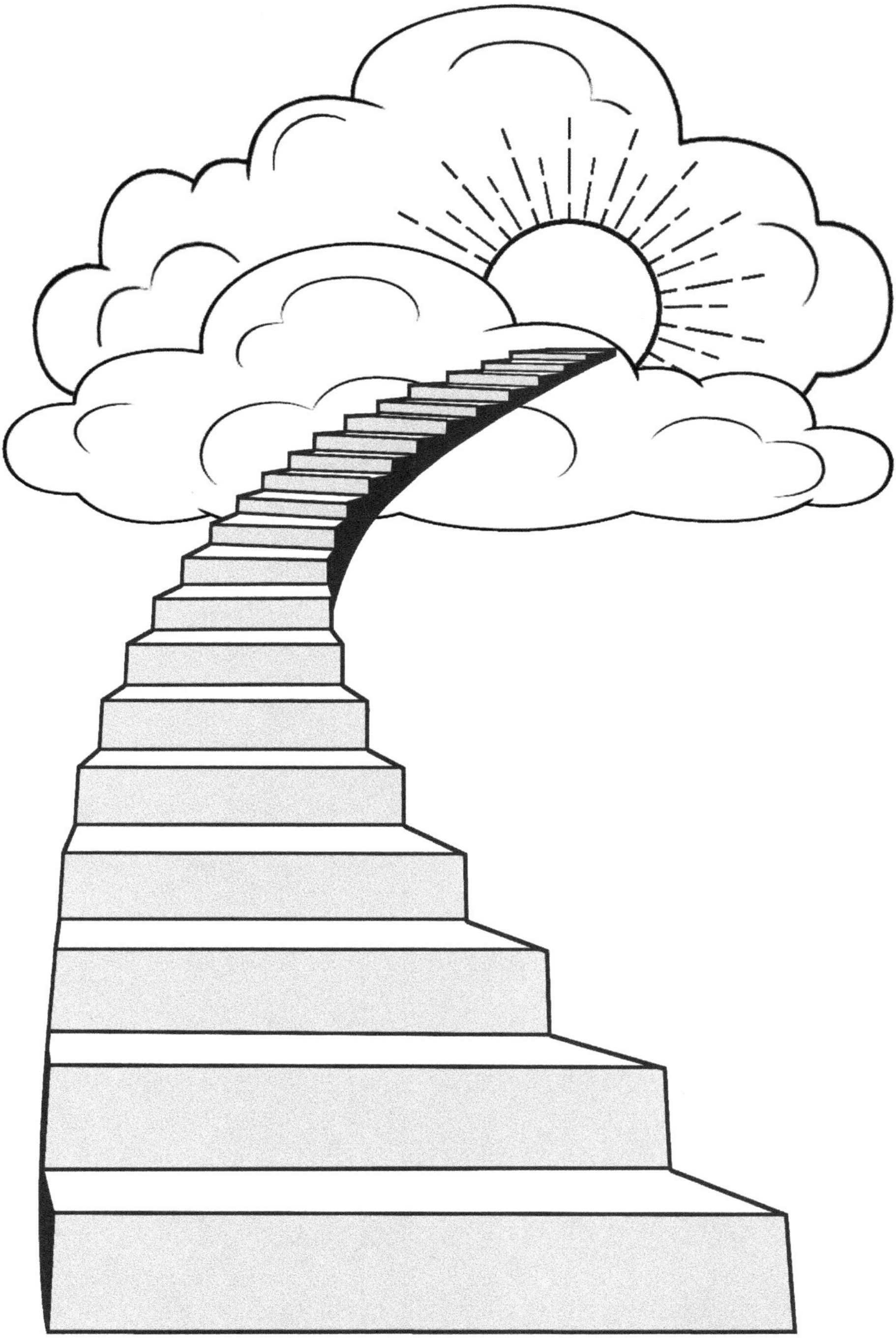

ABOUT THE AUTHOR

Pamela Lawson lives in Glen Burnie, Maryland with her husband, Dave, and their three dogs. She is the mother of two boys, Dalton and Justin, and has two grandchildren, Everleigh and Logan.

Pamela started her Facebook page, Pamela Lawson Poetry at the end of 2019, in hopes to connect with those who need words of encouragement, support, hope, faith, peace and love during their grieving process.

"I have been writing poetry since 2003, a gift I truly believe I was given by God. It is my dream to have my poetry reach as many people as possible to bridge grieving hearts, so they know they are not alone in their grief."

When Pamela isn't writing, she enjoys spending time with her family, her dogs; Harley–a Husky Chow, Token–a Cockapoo mix, and Chase –a Cockapoo, and friends. She also enjoys motorcycle rides with her husband and their friends.

Life is precious and no one knows when it will be their time to be called home.